IMAGES

Commemorating 40 years
of British Transport Films

John Reed

Capital Transport

ISBN 185414 124 4

Published by Capital Transport Publishing, 38 Long Elmes, Harrow Weald, Middlesex

Printed by The KPC Group, Ashford, Kent

Text © John Reed 1990. Photographs © British Rail, British Waterways, London Transport Museum

This book has been published as part of the BTF40 celebrations, sponsored by British Waterways

MOVING IMAGES

Between 1950 and 1986 BTF was the most active industrial film unit in the country producing over 1500 films, commercials, filmstrips and, later on, videos, to help the newly nationalised transport undertakings of Great Britain promote their services and train their staff.

Most people in the UK will have seen a BTF production at some time, because the Unit's work didn't just reflect change and aspiration of the transport world, it also included travel and nature films too. What a transport documentary unit was doing making films about frog spawn, red crested pochards and pussy willows, apart from helping the Unit scoop up over two hundred film awards during its career, is explained in this book.

I owe a lot of thanks to a lot of people, especially to John Legard, John Shearman and Ron Craigen, three key members of BTF from its earliest days, who were happy to give reminiscences and anecdotes, as well as advice, help and time. Also Barry Coward, whose film archive company FAME is custodian of the bulk of BTF's material and who thought it would be a nice idea to commemorate BTF's 40th anniversary with a book, and to Sheila Taylor at the London Transport Museum, which also holds part of the BTF archive.

The initiative with documentary film-making is now with the small screen and with much smaller film units. Let this book be a reminder of the days when the cinema, church hall and mess room played a role in informing and training those eager to be taught and entertained.

Edgar Anstey (1909-1987)

Previous Page **A BTF crew prepares to shoot a sequence in Bristol to illustrate attempts to solve the passenger congestion problem on the City's buses. This was for the film *Work In Progress* (1951).**

Take two cinemas. One a prince among picture palaces in the heart of a capital city, the other a homely centre for entertainment in a bustling provincial port. Unite them briefly on a spring day forty years ago and you have the beginnings of a unique force in documentary film making.

The two unlikely stablemates, the Empire, Leicester Square and the Dorchester Theatre, Hull, were chosen to premiére the first offerings from one of Britain's newest documentary film units, British Transport Films. The date was 19th May 1950, the films, *Transport, Moving House, Inland Waterways* and *Berth 24*. The last of the four explains why Hull was chosen as the second venue, *Berth 24* had been filmed in the city's docks.

A lot has changed in those forty years, especially the conditions under which British Transport Films was created. The first post-war General Election in July 1945, amid some surprise, had resoundingly voted a Labour Government into office with an impressive 146-seat majority. Nationalisation of much of Britain's transport was among the priorities in Labour's manifesto, and within three years the pledge was honoured for on 1st January 1948 the British Transport Commission came into being to oversee the various transport elements which the 1947 Transport Act had embraced. They included the 'big four' railway companies, the Great Western, the LMS, the LNER, and the Southern, which became British Railways; many of the nation's docks, rivers and canals which came under the new Docks and Inland Waterways Executive; London Transport; the Tilling and Scottish Omnibus Groups; and a variety of haulage firms which were united under the title British Road Services.

The Southern Railway, the LMS and London Transport already possessed film units as part of their public relations divisions. LT had begun theirs as recently as 1947, but some had been in existence a lot longer. In 1934 the LMS had shown its legions of staff a newsreel of its prize locomotive 'Royal Scot' touring the USA. This proved so popular that by 1936 the company had converted an old four-wheel carriage into a mobile cinema which travelled all over LMS territory, showing customers and staff informative and image-enhancing railway films. The British Transport Commission, which in effect became the World's biggest employer with 800,000 people working for the organisations under its wing, fortunately viewed the creation of an active film unit an important part of its duty, and in January 1949 announced that one was to be set up. The result was British Transport Films, an amalgamation of what already existed plus the scope to cater for the work of the other bodies now forming part of Britain's very first nationalised transport authority. It was to be the biggest industrial film unit in Britain.

In charge at BTF was renowned documentary film maker Edgar Anstey, a protégé of John Grierson, a pioneer in British documentary films. Before Grierson documentary film making in Britain was all but a blank sheet, except for a handful of nature, medical and scientific films. Newsreels had been made for the cinema since about 1896, Charles Pathé began his newsreel production around 1910, but little existed by way of informative film for general showing. Grierson created the notion of the sponsored documentary, and is even credited with coining the term 'documentary' to describe films which were factual and thought-provoking. In 1928 he made a film about the Scottish fishing industry and called it *Drifters*. The film had a profound effect on young Edgar Anstey. He wrote to Grierson, who was then producer at the Empire Marketing Board, asking for a job and was taken on. Between 1931 and 1934 he worked with Grierson editing scientific and documentary film.

In 1934 Anstey helped set up the Shell Film Unit, and soon after he made two celebrated documentaries, *Housing Problems* and *Enough To Eat*, both highlighting deprivation in mid-thirties Britain. *Housing Problems* provided the first opportunity for victims of social hardship to face a movie camera and speak of their fears.

In 1936 he joined the international documentary film unit 'March of Time' as London Director of Productions, later moving to the Unit's New York office as Foreign Editor. Back in London as the war began he set about producing documentaries for the Government and the Armed Forces. Hostilities over, his work with documentary films continued, first with BOAC and later for an oil company operating in Venezuela.

By 1949 Anstey had built up a creditable reputation in documentary film making, and his expertise was rewarded by an invitation to represent short film production on the Cinematograph Film Council. His impressive cv also made him a likely candidate to take charge of the new British Transport Films production unit then being planned by J. H. Brebner, Chairman of the BTC's Public Relations Co-ordination Committee; he was duly appointed Producer In Charge in May 1949.

Anstey's first task in his new role was quite simply to set up BTF and get it running. In its first year the Unit was based in two locations, London Transport's headquarters in Westminster, and then across the road at 5 Petty France. Eventually it moved into its own premises at 25 Savile Row, in the heart of London's west end. To start with, only a handful of people were employed full time at BTF. The first appointments, Charles Potter (Administration), John Shearman (Assistant Producer), Ron Craigen (Senior Cameraman), James Ritchie (Cameraman) and Ian Ferguson (Production Manager), were joined as the Unit grew by many others including Stewart McAllister, (Supervising Editor) and John Legard (Editor). It says something for Anstey's skill and determination that just a year after the BTF's creation, and two years after the BTC had come into existence, the first batch of films was ready to be shown.

It was Anstey's policy of grooming in-house talent that made the Unit unique in the ever-changing world of film companies. Eventually a team of around 30 in-house professionals, including cameramen, editors, writers and technicians, were working for the Unit full-time. Services and talent still needed importing from outside, to direct, write and compose musical scores for specific films, but in the main the BTF product from the time Anstey began creating the Unit in the summer of 1949 until 1986 when, 700 productions later, it shot its last film, was strictly an in-house affair.

Over the years some distinguished talent emerged. Cameraman David Watkin, who later in his career worked on major movie successes including *Women In Love*, *Sunday, Bloody Sunday*, and more recently *Chariots of*

Fire, began as a trainee with the Unit. He had come from the Southern Railway's film section and expressed a great interest in film making, eventually becoming one of BTF's staff cameramen. Another camera technician who began his career with BTF was Billy Williams. He left during the 1950s to shoot TV commercials before going on to important features like *Gandhi* and *On Golden Pond*. Other notable cameramen on the credits of BTF production were James Ritchie and Robert Paynter. Many of the film scripts were commissioned, but the name Paul Le Saux is often seen on BTF credits as writer. He joined the Unit in 1951, and his unique and varied writing style was ably put to the test on many notable documentaries. Sadly both he and the Chief Editor Stewart McAllister died while still actively involved in BTF work.

Those who remember Anstey from the early BTF days recall an ardent perfectionist who wanted to make films technically excellent. He chose directors whom he knew by reputation were capable of producing quality film. Usually there was a new director for every production to ensure a consistently fresh approach to putting transport issues on the screen. The unending enthusiasm for the job in hand and the abounding family atmosphere are what people who worked for the Unit like to remember most about BTF.

Anstey's job at BTF seemed, on the face of it, straightforward. He had to produce films to acclaim the virtues of Britain's newly nationalised transport industry in all its different forms, encourage people to get out and use it, and provide visual assistance for the training of those who worked for it. Most people in the country thus qualified as BTF audience and the films and film strips produced were designed for showing in cinemas, to clubs, women's institutes, schools and training huts; in fact anywhere where there was a group of potential customers – a formidable challenge, so what could have been Anstey's yardstick for the immense task ahead?

Perhaps it was *Night Mail*, at the time probably the most celebrated documentary with a transport theme. *Night Mail*, made by Harry Watt and Basil Wright for the GPO film unit in 1936, recorded the bustling activity aboard a mail train thundering north to Scotland. But a novel approach with the script, largely made up of verse by the poet W. H. Auden, read to accompanying music composed by Benjamin Britten, caught the imagination, and turned what could so easily have been a mediocre film into one which is still spoken of reverently today. *Night Mail* made people sit up and take notice, and this pioneering treatment of a relatively straightforward topic must have added significantly to documentary film credibility early in the medium's history, setting new standards. In any case Edgar Anstey was proving with his own work that he was an able craftsman capable of making film do the work of several thousand words. His belief that the cinema screen should be used to bring the world to life is evident in much of the material he produced for British Transport Films.

But it wasn't all plain sailing at the beginning. In December 1950 the British Transport Commission was being accused by opposition MPs in the Commons of producing films akin to blatant "political propaganda", and using public money to do it. The film which raised opposition hackles was *Transport*, the first film to bear the BTF name. Although produced by Edgar Anstey it had been made by Pathé under contract to the Unit. The film took a candid look at transport down the years and concluded that most of the problems associated with it were due to past wasteful inter-modal competition. The BTC had arrived to change all that and provide well-managed integrated transport for everyone. The film left people in no doubt why transport in Britain had been nationalised and what the advantages would be. In 1950, with grim memories of Nazi indoctrination techniques in the thirties still fresh in the mind, the word "propaganda" retained an ominous ring. Peter Thorneycroft, then Conservative MP for Monmouth, asked Transport Minister Alfred Barnes to get *Transport* withdrawn from circulation. Mr Barnes refused. He also declined to give a direction to the BTC about the content of future productions.

Parliamentary furore over *Transport* at least proves that Edgar Anstey was shaping up to his task at BTF. *Berth 24* was the first film BTF shot as a unit. This, and the other documentaries screened at BTF's premier event each took an element of the British Transport Commission and showed it working. *Transport* presented an overall picture. *Berth 24* showed typical hectic activity, determined by tides and times, at Hull docks when a passenger and freight steamer, the ss Bravo, berths and prepares for departure following a crossing from Gottenburg. Foreman docker at Hull, George Moore, became a local celebrity when the film was released. He had helped with ideas for the film as it was being shot.

Moving House, made by Public Relations Films for BTF, allayed any fears the potentially gruesome experience might pose by placing the task in the capable hands of experienced and reliable British Road Services staff. The film was given a light hearted treatment by documentary director Richard Massingham, noted for the witty and sympathetic way his films dealt with potentially contentious subjects. The final offering in the quartet was *Inland Waterways*, which promoted commercial use of canals by joining two British Waterways bargees on their regular run from London to Birmingham. It was a good start and the first films received much critical acclaim. It was all summed up by Paul Rotha writing in the July 1950 issue of the magazine *Public Opinion* who said, "Mr Anstey is to be congratulated on the first year's work of his unit. He is creating a new growing point of some of the best of the British documentary makers who have been allowed to idle with frustration and bewilderment for too long".

After the release of the first four titles, which were all public information films, the Unit got down to the business of producing material to satisfy the rest of its BTC remit, which included promotional and training material. For the first decade, and into the sixties, BTF received an annual budget from the British Transport Commission to make its films. But the films didn't just happen, they had to be wanted. To get one produced, member organisations of the British Transport Commission usually approached BTF and specified the type of film required. If they had embarked on a scheme which was going to improve dramatically the service they could offer customers, opened a new facility or wanted to show an aspect of their work which normally went unseen and unappreciated, then a skilfully made film was an ideal medium. Edgar Anstey's role when the initial approach was made was to advise exactly what could be achieved, stressing that film-making was an expensive business. BTF's budget was quite small, being roughly equivalent to the cost of buying one new diesel locomotive a year, and use of the money had to be justified. But once Anstey was satisfied a project was worthwhile he gave it his full commitment and backing.

This rather cosy arrangement lasted until the British Transport Commission was wound up by the 1962 Transport Act. After this BTF, which continued to thrive under the wing of British Railways PR Department at BR's Melbury House Headquarters in London's Marylebone, began running its affairs on more commercial lines. On the face of it not very much altered after 1962. BTF, still with Edgar Anstey in charge, continued to produce documentaries for the former BTC Group members, although now they had to pay for what they commissioned. The new arrangements allowed BTF to make films in association with other organisations like the British Tourist Authority. By the early 1970s video was being used, particularly in staff training, and BTF had its own electronic production unit.

Edgar Anstey retired in 1974 and John Shepherd, from Admiralty, took the helm. But the work continued. BTF even made some TV commercials for BR, pitching for the work alongside advertising agencies. The Unit's own film library was expanded in 1975 to become the Transport and Travel Film Library, embracing transport visual aids from many national and international organisations. On its shelves were films, filmstrips and videos from organisations as diverse as the Electricity Council and Italian State Railways. But already things were changing. The initiative for documentary film making had passed to television. As the cost-cutting 1980s progressed, and with more independent film production companies coming on the scene, the need for an in-house film facility at BR diminished. In 1981 BTF's film library closed and the material was offered back to the respective owners. For a time British Rail's and London Transport's was marketed by the Central Office of Information. The remnants of BTF continued to assist in film and video production, chiefly for British Rail, until 1986 when things finally came to an end. Edgar Anstey died the following year.

The very last film to bear the BTF logo was produced in a very different political climate to the first batch in 1950, but appropriately it looked to a future where public transport, or at any rate the railways, would be playing a key role. The film was *Tomorrow's Way* (1986), and it predicted a time when a journey from Manchester to Paris by train without a change would be more than just a pipe dream, courtesy of the Channel Tunnel.

It's not easy to condense 36 years of film making into a slim volume without leaving something out. So what follows is a brief trawl through the BTF years to present an idea of the different types of films made by the Unit and fish out some of the highlights in a career which was crowned by the success of winning well over 200 film awards including a much coveted Oscar.

Transfer of allegiance. British Railways' new lion and wheel symbol heralds the dawn of a new era on the country's rail services, and by 1950 when it was featured being applied to a locomotive's tender in BTF's first film *Transport* was a familiar sight on virtually every engine in BR's fleet.

Meanwhile the BTC influence was altering the appearance of Britain's lorries and barges as well.

BTF's PUBLIC RELATIONS FILMS

BTF adopted various approaches to projecting positive messages about the way British transport worked and how it was developing for the nation's good. Drama, humour, surprise, but above all information and facts, were all there in appropriate measure depending on the story being told.

British Railways was to remain BTF's biggest customer from its early years right until the Unit ceased to function in 1986. During the first year or so it was mainly training films that BR commissioned from the Unit. The first production made specifically to inform the public at large what an onerous task it was to provide railway services was *Train Time* (1952) which showed what was involved in moving freight and passengers to and from an assortment of locations the length and breadth of the country. Two years later BTF made *Elizabethan Express*, now regarded as a classic of its kind, for BR. The film takes us on a 393-mile non-stop summertime journey from London to Edinburgh behind class A4 Pacific locomotive 'Silver Fox', showing on the way something of the part played by individual BR staff in preparing the train for its journey northward; the wheel tappers, shunters, signalmen and plate layers, all of whom along with those actually on the train, driver, fireman, guard, and buffet staff, have contributed something essential toward making the trip run smoothly and safely. The message is nicely wrapped in a commentary composed in verse, perhaps under the inspiration of *Night Mail*, by BTF's staff writer Paul Le Saux. The film begins with the preparations to depart, and the cast of characters being introduced:

"Ron Marrable, top link train driver,
who's always a punctual arriver
wears boots, footplate size,
has colour-light eyes
and engine oil in his saliva."

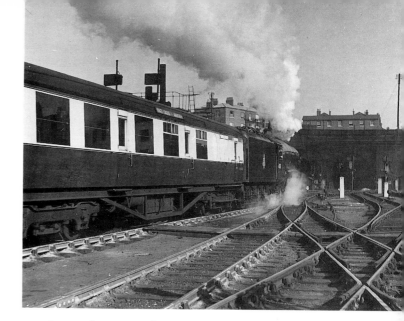

Later, after a crew change at York the time has slipped a bit:

"But now the express has lost time she'll be late
unless Driver Tony and Mungo his mate
can make up four minutes and nearly a quarter
on the difficult stretch running over the border."

The verses are spoken alternately by the actors Howard Marion Crawford and Alan Wheatley, which adds remarkably to the strong feeling of movement already achieved by the camera techniques used to record the train in motion.

13

Of course trains are only a part of the railway service mix. There is the infrastructure too, stations, bridges, track and tunnels, all to be maintained to the highest standards possible. Many films were produced to illustrate the importance of good order behind the scenes. *Groundwork For Progress* (1959) showed Civil Engineering tasks being carried out on tracks and bridges as part of BR's modernisation programme, referring to the opportunities modernisation had created for young Civil Engineers. *Freight And A City* (1966) told of how BR had completely remodelled its goods operations in Sheffield, centred on a new complex of marshalling yards, a diesel locomotive maintenance depot and freight terminal. The reconstruction of Robert Stephenson's Britannia Bridge across the Menai Strait, almost destroyed by fire in 1970, was the subject of *Britannia – A Bridge* (1975). *Operation London Bridge* (1975) was about reconstructing a busy main line rail terminal.

By the late-1950s BR's far-reaching modernisation programme was under way. This prompted a series of films entitled *Report On Modernisation* which began in 1959 and continued until 1965 when it was renamed *Rail Report*. In its new guise it covered topics as diverse as the new Motorail terminal at Olympia, a hot axle box detector, and new trains for the Bournemouth Line. A series in a similar newsreel style, but this time made especially for staff, was *The Way Ahead*, which contained short topical items of national and regional interest. The series, made between 1962 and 1964, was very time consuming, and proved a drain on BTF resources during the period the Unit was moving from the BTC era to being a more commercial outfit.

More weighty topics deserved full-length documentary treatment. Subject matter could vary from the electrification of the busy Liverpool Street to Southend (Victoria) line *Service For Southend* (1957), to an examination of the way BR was meeting the problems created by the changing pattern of coal distribution, *Trains – Not Wagons* (1964). A favourite topic for the PR film was a new service. *Blue Pullman* (1960) unveiled the latest 90mph diesel trains then coming in on routes from London. The film had no commentary; instead the story was told through snatches of conversation during crew training and passenger inspection of the stylish new trains and their facilities. At the other end of the scale, pieces of equipment usually taken for granted were given the limelight. No prizes for the hidden message in *I Am A Litter Basket* (1959). By the seventies British Rail, as it was then called, was up front with new technology. It was the time of containerisation, the subject of several films, including *Freight Flow* (1969) which traced the development of the Freightliner service showing how the new systems could overcome a multitude of problems experienced when shipping freight by other means. Novel invention Hovercraft were featured in *Seaspeed Story* (1970), skimming across the waves on BR's Seaspeed services to the Isle of Wight and the Continent.

Hovering above its rippling green carpet the 38-seater SRN6 Hovercraft begins its 20-minute journey from Southampton to Cowes in a scene from *Seaspeed Story* (1970).

Enter *The Blue Pullman*, subject of a 1960 BTF PR documentary which showed staff being trained to operate the 90mph machines, as well as giving a glimpse of some of the amenities for passengers to enjoy on board.

Facing Page **No expense was spared in filming *Blue Pullman*. A cameraman perches on the flank of a helicopter on hire to BTF, as the machine hovers alongside the moving train.**

This Page **1967, the dawn of BR's new image. The film *Rail* was a celebration of a new era with rhythmically edited scenes imaginatively set to music by Wilfred Josephs. The new age was represented by electric traction.**

Another landmark in the list of PR films made for BR came in 1961, the year when an estimated 5½ million people watched at least one BTF production. The acclaimed new film was *Terminus*, a day in the life of London's busiest commuter station, Waterloo. It was directed by John Schlesinger, who later went on to direct major box office successes of the calibre of *Darling*, *Billy Liar*, and *Sunday, Bloody Sunday*. The content of *Terminus* was succinctly summed up by BTF's own catalogue at the time which warned potential viewers they would witness, " . . . grief and joy, meeting and parting, high comedy and near tragedy". In many earlier BTF productions featuring staff or passengers, actors were often used, usually to good effect, and much of the ensuing action was carefully orchestrated. Such was the case with *This Is York* made eight years before *Terminus*, when every foot of film was planned in advance.

But Schlesinger was seeking realism with *Terminus*. Before filming began he spent days and days just wandering around Waterloo station, sitting in cafeterias and waiting rooms, and joining the police on their nightly patrols. Shooting took three weeks, and editing six months. The whole thing cost £10,000. The result won BTF fourteen awards, including the Grand Prix at the 1961 Venice Film Festival. In one memorable scene a small boy, lost and bewildered in the giant station, is comforted by staff trying to find his mother. How better to inject that extra spark of reality than to actually persuade the mother to "lose" her son, a relative of Schlesinger's, for ten minutes without the child's knowledge? This Schlesinger did.

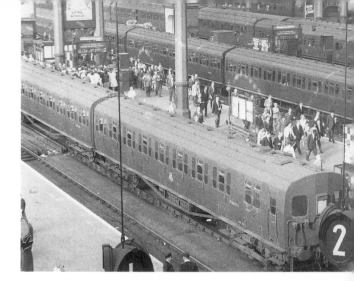

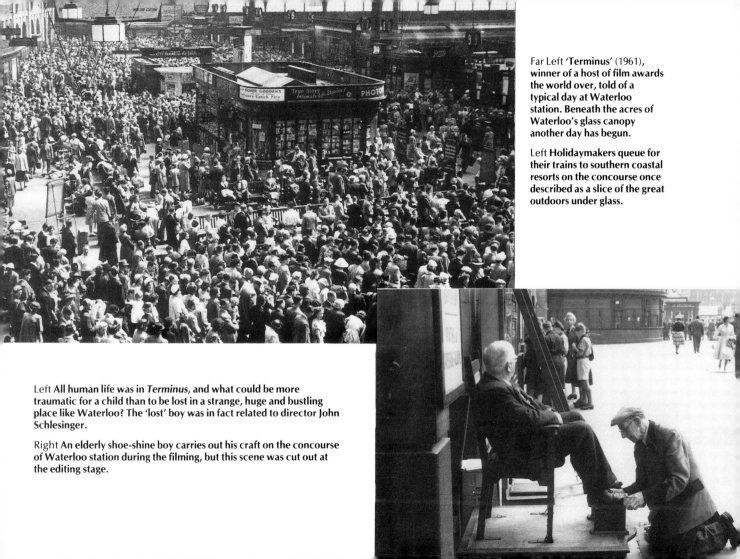

Far Left 'Terminus' (1961), winner of a host of film awards the world over, told of a typical day at Waterloo station. Beneath the acres of Waterloo's glass canopy another day has begun.

Left Holidaymakers queue for their trains to southern coastal resorts on the concourse once described as a slice of the great outdoors under glass.

Left All human life was in *Terminus*, and what could be more traumatic for a child than to be lost in a strange, huge and bustling place like Waterloo? The 'lost' boy was in fact related to director John Schlesinger.

Right An elderly shoe-shine boy carries out his craft on the concourse of Waterloo station during the filming, but this scene was cut out at the editing stage.

Snow Drift At Bleath Gill (1955) and a marooned goods train is finally rescued by snow plough four days after becoming stranded.

Acts of heroic achievement and outstanding organisation warranted public attention too and many came under the scrutiny of BTF's camera. One such, *Snow Drift At Bleath Gill* (1955) witnessed a snowbound freight train being dug out of a frozen drift. Several other films recorded specific events for posterity, like Royal visits, *A Queen's Day* (1974), and *Centenary Express* (1980), which celebrated 100 years of on-train catering. Naturally, Britain's railway history was catered for in many films, *Giants Of Steam* (1963), *The Great Highway* (1965) and *Rail 150* (1975); all helped to impress upon audiences that apart from being an efficient and forward-looking provider of transport, British Rail proudly recognised its important heritage.

This Is York (1953) focussed on activity in and around York station including the signal control room, then one of the most modern in the world, and of course the station itself, looking strangely deserted in a brief mid-morning lull between trains.

Left **Children often featured in BTF productions making full use of transport and enjoying it in the process. Another scene from *This Is York*, but hasn't someone forgotten to give the ticket collector a more up to date cap to wear?**

Above **'Single to Lewes, Guv? Third Class? Thirteen and ten please.' The customer pays with a ten bob note and coin. Such a lot has changed in forty years. Card tickets have all but disappeared, third class travel on BR is long gone and 13/10d now masquerades as 69p.**

Snow clad hills and frost bleached ground make the movement of a goods train all the more prominent in this scene from *Fully Fitted Freight* (1957)

A coal train departs Duffryn Rhondda Colliery, from *Bridge of Song* (1955).

Below Left **In a corner of Southampton Docks, an American built 0-6-0 tank engine, one of 14 acquired by the Southern Railway from the War Department in 1947, hauls cargo from the quayside.**

Below **The old Woodhead tunnel on the Manchester to Sheffield main line was collapsing before the war, and replacement soon became an urgent task. The LNER film of the tunnel construction was not finished by the time BTF took over in 1949. BTF re-shot much of the film and released it as *Signpost* in 1955 to herald the changes to come under the newly published Modernisation Report.**

Above *Wires Over The Border* (1974) was an account, in human and non-technical terms, of the electrification of BR's West Coast mainline. Staff on the Civil and Mechanical Engineer's hybrid train fix the overhead to the supports in a suitably rugged location, while building of the class 87 electric locomotives designed to work on the line proceeds at BREL.

Left The work of the British Railways' materials stores merited a documentary of its own in 1954, *What's In Store?* All materials have a purpose and some were shown being used to make an end product, in this case a new railway carriage at York.

Facing Page A look into a miniature crystal ball came with *Modelling For The Future* (1961). In it the age-old dream of a rail tunnel beneath the Channel connecting England and France was scaled down to its possibilities.

Left 'My umbrella's the one with a black handle, you'll not miss it!' Lost property in the bowels of London Transport's Baker Street Lost Property Office waiting for an owner, and a very similar scene at Waterloo BR.

Above Before the jet age, boat trains connected with ships of all lines. Names such as Union Castle, United States, Shaw Saville, Royal Mail, and Home Lines are now just echo's of grander days. Finger boards wait in a rack at Waterloo.

Above Left **Shunting a 'steam banana' during the night in Derby on the *Fully Fitted Freight* over night service from Bristol to Leeds.** A 'steam banana' was an enclosed van heated by the hot steam from the locomotive so that green bananas ripened during their journey.

Above **A Guard gives the clear signal from his goods brake and the *Fully Fitted Freight* express edges out of Derby for Leeds.**

THOMASON

Left **Gresley-designed 4-6-0 No.61006 relegated from express passenger to a night freight train.** As diesels took over passenger trains on British Railways, these once great engines found themselves relegated to such duties.

London Transport was not entirely new to the world of documentary films, having created its own film service just a year before BTF was formed. It had already commissioned and made films. One, *Moving Millions* (1948) provided the first moving testament to the work of LT. It was followed by a series called *Cine Gazette* originally produced by London Transport, but taken over by BTF from 1950. The Gazettes were newsreel style productions containing two or three unrelated items but each important in its own right. Many different aspects of London Transport's activity were covered by the Gazettes. Each was vital to the successful running of Britain's largest urban transport undertaking, so why shouldn't LT's legions of customers be told about them? Items ranged from tube train overhaul to lost property, and from testing wider buses to the lubrication of trolleybus overhead wiring. Even rock cake production at the Croydon Canteen Food Production Centre got an airing! Some items from the Gazettes even found their way onto BBC TV Children's Television as early as March 1952.

Scenes from *Moving Millions*, predecessor of the Cine Gazette series handled by BTF for London Transport in the 1950s. Football crowds alight at Wembley Park; rush hour crowds meet a train arriving at a station on the Central Line.

Moving Millions was a testament in celluloid to the work of the world's biggest urban transport undertaking. Derby Day is over at Epsom, but LT's race to get the punters home is only just beginning.

Throughout LT's Last Tram Week, in July 1952, a BTF unit cruised around south London recording scenes for posterity. The result, *The Elephant Will Never Forget*, one of the most popular films in BTF's catalogue. In Beresford Square, Woolwich, market shoppers jostle with buses, trolleybuses and, for a few more hours, trams, clanging and swaying across the cobbles.

No vacant seats on this last day trip, not even for a babe in arms.

Without doubt the most famous Cine Gazette of all is number 12, "The Elephant Will Never Forget" released in 1953. This one-subject Gazette told the story of the last week of London's trams the previous July. It doesn't fit easily into the accepted PR category unless the change could be deemed progress, and in 1952 replacing what was then regarded as an outdated mode of transport was certainly progress. So this heap of nostalgia is more of a historical record than anything else, showing a much loved element of transport passing into history. *Elephant* has proved to be one of BTF's most popular productions but apparently when it was made its director, John Krish, was criticised for over-shooting on what was considered a minor production.

Above Right **'In thirty six hours he'll be a bus driver, and for the first time in forty two years he'd be sitting down.'**

Right **Revellers on the very last London tram listen to LT's Chairman, standing somewhere below in the mêlée at New Cross depot, deliver the obligatory 'farewell old trams' speech.**

With the ending of the Cine Gazette series in 1956 BTF's PR material for London Transport took on a more conventional form. LT was still anxious to illustrate the complex nature of its activities, and these were ably displayed in *Overhaul* (1956), which peeped behind the gigantic doors of Aldenham, the world's largest bus overhaul works, *Under Night Streets* (1958) which revealed the intense subterranean maintenance work undertaken on the Underground at night beginning immediately after the last tube train had returned to its depot, and *All That Mighty Heart* (1963). This film, a day in the life of London Transport, used an ingeneous technique. No commentary, just signature tunes and snippets from popular BBC radio and TV programmes of the period which, by having an unmistakable time association like *Housewives' Choice* and *Music While You Work*, helped to put the hour of the day in context right from the first morning train gliding out of its depot, to the twinkling lights of the last bus disappearing across Waterloo Bridge. 1963 was also the year London's underground railway celebrated it centenary. The occasion was marked by *A Hundred Years Underground*, a 40-minute documentary made in association with the BBC, which was shown on TV the following year.

The giant body shop at London Transport's Aldenham bus overhaul works, scene of *Overhaul* (1956). Over 40 completely renovated buses emerged weekly from the factory. The film was one of the first non-promotional BTF documentaries shot in colour.

Facing Page **The Victoria Line story proceeds with the building of its rolling stock at Metro-Cammell's Birmingham factory, despite the presence of a BTF film crew.**

London Transport's achievements during the BTF era reached a peak with the building of the Victoria Line, the first completely new tube railway in London for sixty years. The construction and commissioning of the Line was faithfully recorded on film at every stage, and gave one unit at BTF six full years of work. Hardly a week passed without some attendance by BTF camera crews at the digging face deep below the capital. Resident engineers on site let the unit know when something interesting, such as a tunnel breakthrough, was going to happen, and the cameras started rolling. The result was a series of update documentaries, five in all, each giving a full account of progress. The work culminated in a 45-minute colour feature, *London's Victoria Line* (1969) which proved to be British Transport Film's largest production in terms of time, manpower, footage and cost.

London's Underground never sleeps, despite the last trains running soon after midnight. This man emerging from the depths of Piccadilly Circus station booking hall has been cleaning ducting in the early hours. Next stop — Bath? A scene from *Under Night Streets* (1958)

Prior to the introduction of 8ft wide buses in London, two of these test vehicles were built. In a scene from an early *Cine Gazette* film produced for London Transport, one of the vehicles is being overtaken by a trolleybus just over a mile south of the Aldenham works where it was normally kept.

The other organisations which made up the British Transport Commission were equally anxious to promote a strong image. Bus operators in the BTC group perhaps benefited from the content of *Away For The Day* (1952); groups of elderly ladies treating themselves to a day out, and of course a cream tea, in the countryside by hiring coaches from BTC-owned bus companies. British Road Services commissioned BTF to produce several documentaries about road haulage, and once again anything out of the ordinary was usually seized upon as being prime material for a film. An early example was *Dodging the Column* (1952) which left the viewer in no doubt as to the skill and forward planning involved in moving a 137-foot distillation column the 500 miles by road from Greenwich in London to Grangemouth in Scotland. The commentary is spoken by actors purporting to be involved in driving and manouevring the monster to its destination, once again a novel departure from the usual treatment meted out on countless mundane documentaries from other sources produced during the same period. In 1958 BRS moved a 200-ton transformer from Hayes in Middlesex to Iver in Buckinghamshire. It was the subject of another film, *Giant Load*. Not such a long journey this time, but one which required considerable planning and precision right up until the grey lump was successfully deposited in its new home.

Facing Page **Through the streets of London rumbles 'the column' on its way to Scotland. *Dodging The Column* (1952) accompanied it on its tentative trip.**

Above *Away For The Day* (1952) followed groups of day trippers from an assortment of locales on days out around the country. This group seem full of anticipation at the start of their day away from a rather bleak Abercwmboi.

BTF produced several films for British Rail promoting its rapidly expanding container freight service, Freightliner. The ease of handling and loading for onward transportation was very much to the fore, as was the swift transportation between depots/ports.

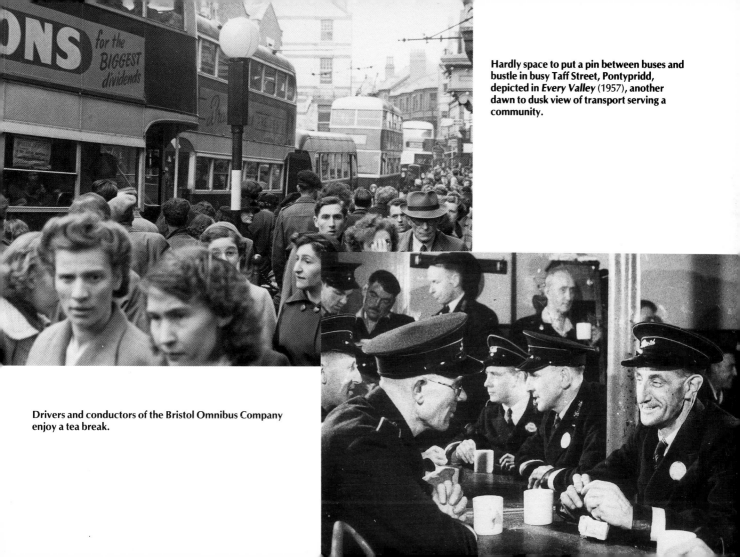

Hardly space to put a pin between buses and bustle in busy Taff Street, Pontypridd, depicted in *Every Valley* (1957), another dawn to dusk view of transport serving a community.

Drivers and conductors of the Bristol Omnibus Company enjoy a tea break.

Finally the Docks and Inland Waterways Executive, which took charge of the most historic and in some cases most picturesque aspect of the BTC, commissioned some excellent short public relations films about life in Britain's water transport industry, the Docks and canals. One of the very first, *Berth 24*, was followed in 1952 by *Ocean Terminal* about life in Southampton Docks. At the time Southampton was the destination of many of the world's largest ocean-going passenger liners, including the Atlantic Queens, and the film focussed on some of the people who made the whole operation buzz, a tugboat skipper, a ship's stewardess, a baggage handler, a

'. . . it's off to work they go'. **Hull dockers arrive for another day's labour at *Berth 24* (1950).**

Facing Page **The tiny tug 'Waterman' is dwarfed by cargo ships.**

pilotman, and a taxi driver. Some films, like *Timber Move* (1965), majored on efficient cargo handling in docks. In a slightly paradoxical vein *Give Your Car A Holiday* (1967) showed how ferry services and the ports were adapting to the task of catering for the growing popularity in holiday cross-water car traffic, something which was helping to kill off rail transport to the ferry terminals.

Inland waterway traffic was the oldest transport element in the BTC sphere. Even at the dawn of the juggernaught and containerisation, narrowboats and barges were still gently moving their cargoes between towns on canals and rivers in much the same was as they had done for decades past, and they made picturesque film stars. Commercial narrowboats were represented by *Inland Waterways* at BTF's first show, and other films followed. *There Go The Boats* (1952) surveyed nearly 200 years of Britain's canals emphasising their essential role in contemporary Britain's transport structure, as well as looking at their potential for leisure activity too. At the end of the decade *Broad Waterways* (1959) looked again at Britain's canal and river industry, this time poised for modernisation and development, all built around a two-day barge journey carrying newsprint between Hull docks and Nottingham along the River Trent. In 1970 BTF made its last film for British Waterways *The World of Waterways*, a round-up of the variety of activities on the the nation's canal network, from cargo transportation to leisure. The British Waterways continued to produce films about inland waterways but after 1970 commissioned them from other sources.

BTF sometimes co-operated with other organisations in

Car ferries became popular in the sixties and seventies. Life aboard was depicted as being carefree and relaxing and in no time at all you were on the other side being greeted by smiling customs officials.

the production of documentaries. The Post Office joined forces with the Unit to make *Thirty Million Letters* in 1963. The film wasn't a rehash of *Night Mail*, as more conventional GPO work was featured. But on-train letter sorting was included as was the automatic mail bag collector which caught sacks of mail from fast moving trains into a net for onward transportation by van. *John Betjamin Goes by Train*, *Water Buds*, *Plumb Loco*, *A Hundred Years Underground* and *Giants Of Steam* were made in association with the BBC and shown on television.

Right at the end of the fifties the colour film *Broad Waterways* looked forward to a rosy future for the commercial development of Britain's canals and rivers. At Hull Docks, 110 tons of newsprint from Finland is loaded onto the barge 'Thames'. Then it's off, along the River Trent for a two day sail to Nottingham. Within ten years BTF was making films about containerisation at Britain's major ports, a new kind of industrial revolution which was to usher in a period of decline for the canals.

Sunset over Harwich looking towards Parkeston Quay the berth for the train ferries from Zeebrugge featured in *Linkspan*. This film, named after the lifting bridge which connects the ferries to dry land, portrayed a typical day on the boats. The two Trinity House lightships in the foreground and the sailing barge in the distance are now things of the past.

An assortment of cars queue to board a cross-Channel ferry in 1956. Back then most of the ferries sailed under the BR flag. Two BMC soft tops, a Morris Minor and Austin Somerset, give the setting a fifties flavour added to by an American Buick, the occupants 'doing Europe' perhaps. Aboard the Hampton ferry the travellers head for open Channel and Continent as Dover's White Cliffs slip gently past.

Left *Ocean Terminal* (1951). The huge Atlantic liner 'Queen Elizabeth', setting sail for New York, dwarfs the little tug 'Calshot' assisting in the operation.

Right The tug 'Zetland' steers a Russian ship into the newly mechanised Grangemouth Docks on the Firth of Forth, subject of a BTF film made in 1962.

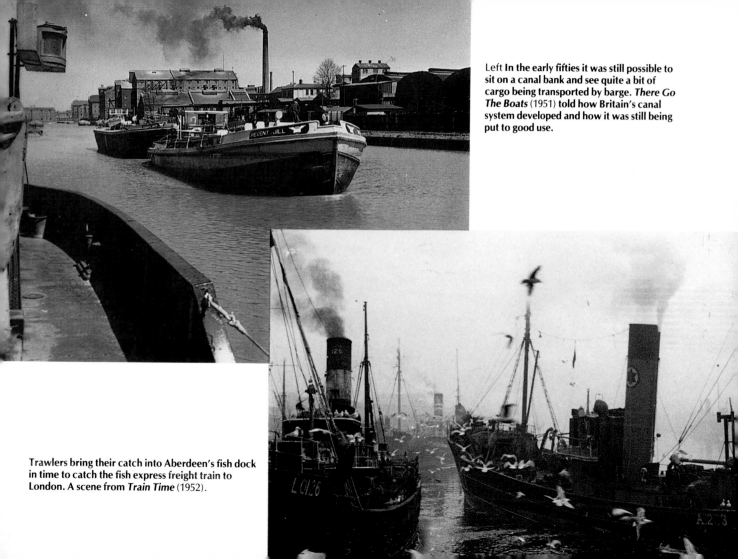

Left **In the early fifties it was still possible to sit on a canal bank and see quite a bit of cargo being transported by barge. *There Go The Boats*** (1951) **told how Britain's canal system developed and how it was still being put to good use.**

Trawlers bring their catch into Aberdeen's fish dock in time to catch the fish express freight train to London. A scene from *Train Time* (1952).

THE TRAINING FILMS

In 1956 BTF released *Making Tracks*, a 17-minute PR film revealing how technology, in the shape of mobile cranes, was revolutionising the essential chore of railway renewal. The film provides a useful bridge between the public relations documentary and another vital role of BTF, producing staff training films, for *Making Tracks* had started life as a training film for track maintenance staff *Mechanised Renewal Of Plain Line*.

Training material accounted for roughly 60% of BTF's total output down the years, the films mostly having a strong railway bias in being made principally for British Railways and London Transport. Effective training of staff was also evident in some of the PR documentaries, no doubt to reassure customers that they were in capable and steady hands when travelling with a nationalised transport undertaking. Although the training films were never designed for public showing, their audiences could be just as critical, so the material had to be of a high standard. A well-trained and enthusiastic staff is as crucial an element in transport as in any other business, perhaps more so. The films thus had to command attention as well as be entertaining and so here, as in other areas of BTF's work, Edgar Anstey employed similar techniques, creative concepts complemented in many instances by good camera work and well written commentaries read by professional actors.

In a way the training films are among the most interesting in BTF's catalogue because a lot of long forgotten pieces of transport equipment and working practices are examined in detail. Certainly most aspects of railway operation on both British Railways and the London Underground were covered, from driving trains to laying and maintaining track, and from signalling to keeping a courteous eye on passengers. Many films put the spotlight on the ever-important area of safety when working on the railway. Just to peruse the long list of titles suggests the range of topics the films embraced. *Track Buckling And Its Prevention* (1951), *Power Signal Lineman* (1952), *Measured Packing* (1953), *Driving Technique* (1964), *Courtesy* (1964), and *Safety Precautions On Electrified Lines* (1964); all studied specific areas of work, and because in essence many of the tasks didn't alter from one year to the next the films were still being shown to staff in training huts and workshops many years after they were made.

It was in the sphere of training where in 1970 BTF took its first steps into the fast growing world of video. This was with a series called "Workshop Safety" and it ushered in a new era of training visual aids. The purpose was to show BR staff working in large railway workshops, like Crewe and Derby, how they could improve their own safety. As with ordinary film-making, a complete production unit including two cameramen and technicians, descended on a specified workshop and within a couple of days a 10-15 minute safety video training film, featuring the works' own safety officers, had been made for showing at special sessions to all staff all around the works.

A training film of special interest is *The Third Sam* (1962), a 10-minute look at how the different character traits of fledgling electric train driver, Sam Smith, are called upon to help him deal with a train failure. The commentary was written as a monologue by director Ken Fairbairn, and delivered in typically authoritative fashion by the comic actor Stanley Holloway. Such treatment took the film away from the "now this is what you do next" category and gave it greater impact.

And impact is certainly something you need when warning children of the dangers of trespassing on railway lines. BTF made several films with this intention as the problem grew worse in the sixties and seventies. One of the first was *The Railway Story* (1964), which featured pop singer Joe Brown telling children how to be more safety conscious on the railway. In 1967 *Crossing The Railway Safely* was made to coincide with the introduction of new half-barrier crossings which were then replacing the traditional gates. Commentary was spoken by Leslie Crowther, who at the time compéred 'Crackerjack' on children's TV. Familiar faces helped to gain attention and confidence. In contrast *The Finishing Line* (1976) used shock tactics, staging a mock school sports day on a busy railway line complete with all the carnage such a harebrained scheme would induce. The film received a hostile reception from the teaching profession when it was first shown due to the quite violent treatment of some of the scenes. It had a relatively short life as a result and was replaced in 1980 by *Robbie*; what happens to a little boy who ventures onto the railway track to retrieve a football. *Robbie* was made in three versions covering different types of track and train operation, and is still being shown in schools in 1990.

BTF produced an impressive selection of filmstrips during the 1950s and early 1960s. They paralleled the general film material in subject and content. Filmstrips could be loaned by clubs for showing on special projectors. Did any Townswomen's Guild hire *Clearances* (1956), a filmstrip about bridge heights? In this frame an ex-Great Western pannier tank demonstrates the Ministry of Transport's desired structure gauge for single-track lines.

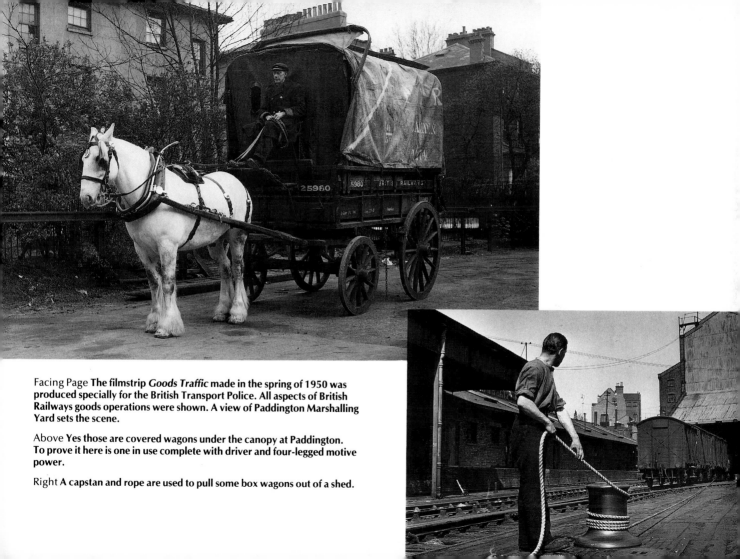

Facing Page **The filmstrip *Goods Traffic* made in the spring of 1950 was produced specially for the British Transport Police. All aspects of British Railways goods operations were shown. A view of Paddington Marshalling Yard sets the scene.**

Above **Yes those are covered wagons under the canopy at Paddington. To prove it here is one in use complete with driver and four-legged motive power.**

Right **A capstan and rope are used to pull some box wagons out of a shed.**

BTF's documentary *Long Night Haul* about nighttime lorry driving had a filmstrip companion *Night Truck Driver* (1956). Having clocked on at a London BRS depot and collected his load the driver steers his charge through the western suburbs in the early evening. But the journey isn't without incident. The lorry develops engine trouble which, of course, the highly trained BRS driver is easily able to fix, but it causes a delay. He rings his destination to warn them he'll be late.

Facing Page **A trolley loaded with urgent ships' stores being taken from a service lift at Waterloo and steered towards a waiting train. A still from training film strip *Railway Parcels Traffic*.**

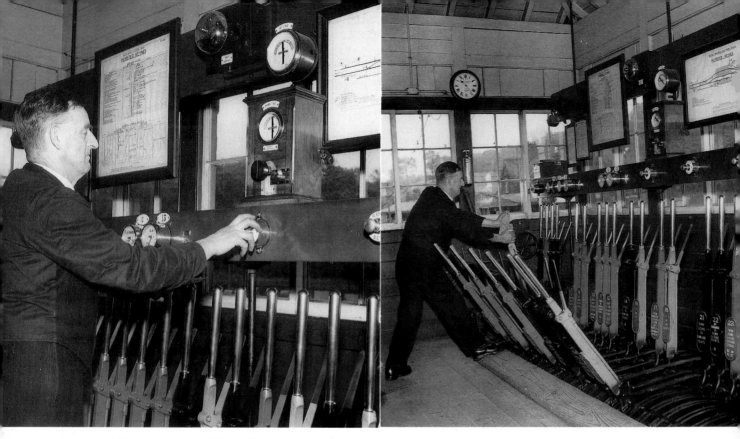

Training material forms a large part of the BTF filmstrips archive, after all could a strip called *Headway Margins* be used for anything else? It shows how a signalman accepts and records a train. The signal box at Horsted Keynes was used for the photography. In 1955, when the strip was made, the box was in daily use on BR's East Grinstead to Lewes line; and it's still used today, helping to regulate the trains on the Bluebell Railway, which the line became when privately purchased for preservation in 1960.

Electric points, or rather the detection of faults with them using special apparatus, probably caused no worries to BR signal engineers after the complex operation was explained in a 1962 filmstrip. In this still the points are being hand-cranked to normal position, while a ⅛inch gauge is inserted in the junction of the two rails. The film was made at King's Cross.

Shepton Mallet on the old Somerset and Dorset Joint Railway was the setting for a training film on the very important subject of a single-track working. A red barrier protected by detonators is a visible reminder for vigilance.

Below A pilotman, riding in the cab of BR standard class 4-6-0 75071, warns a crossing keeper of the situation.

Catch points secured, a ganger with a red flag gives the clear signal to the driver of ex-SDJR 2-8-0 No.53810 as it crosses back to the proper tracks.

THE PROMOTIONAL FILMS

"March, and winter is still in the woods.
This is the moment of pause between the seasons.
The tilting turn of the year.
Under a thin cold sun lie the spectres of last year's summer.
The relics of braken, rosebay and bullrush.
But in the stillness of wood and pond,
Spring and a new year are already stirring."

These lyrically observant lines, by the author and poet Laurie Lee, introduce us to a *Journey Into Spring* (1957), a colourful look at a Hampshire countryside slowly awakening after the harshness of winter. The stars are the plants and small animals found around the parish of Selborne, once the home of the Reverend Gilbert White, a naturalist who two centuries ago recorded how flora and fauna changed with the seasons. Laurie Lee's vivid and beautiful commentary read in soft tones by the actor Stephen Murray to accompanying film shot by Paddy Carey, set to music by Edward Williams, serve to create a masterpiece. Some tricks of the trade were used to present pond life; samples were taken from the pond near the village and filmed in a tank at Haslemere Museum. At the time the film was criticised in some quarters for being too pretty and undynamic, but *Journey Into Spring* repaid the time, effort and creative enthusiasm put into it by winning a BAFTA award for Best Documentary in 1957.

Journey Into Spring is a nature film, pure and simple. There's no mention of transport. Not a train or coach intrudes on the serenity so skilfully brought to the screen by director Ralph Keene, a maker of documentary films since 1934. So why was it made? Simply, like all BTF's promotional and nature films, to promote transport as a means to an end. The "end" might be an historic city or town, a wedge of peaceful, picturesque countryside, or a stretch of salty fresh coastline. From 1952, when the first transport promotional film, *The Heart Is Highland* was released, BTF crafted many excellent travelogues, all filmed in colour, and all with the purpose of enticing people out of their armchairs, away from familiar surroundings, and off to other parts of the country. If a change of scene was the remedy, transport to it was the prescribed tonic.

The message is loudly proclaimed in *London's Country* (1954), "The hills, the woods, the rivers are waiting. Ignore them and any child will say you're a stay at home, down in the drain, tarmac and stone will crush your brain". So says Paul Le Saux's elegantly effusive script, persuasively delivered by the actor Howard Marion Crawford, leaving little doubt as to the underlying message of the film. Get away from the bustle of the city, just for a short while, to sustain your sanity. The film displays in vivid Technicolor a host of places in the Home Counties which could be visited and enjoyed in a day from London by train, bus, tube or Green Line coach.

BTF cast its net far and wide for travelogue locations. In the end almost very region in Britain had been committed to celluloid. The films either homed in on specific areas, showed people enjoying particular outdoor activities, or coaxed them away from home, even for a few hours. One of the latter was *A Day Of One's Own* (1955) which showed how housewives from different parts of the country chose to spend a day away from the daily round of domestic chores. This could prove a taster for trips further afield, and there was no shortage of suggestions from BTF. Once again a glance through BTF's catalogue, and the 1969 edition lists over 60 travelogues and nature films, gives an idea. Why not take a *West Country Journey*, go *Down To Sussex*, enjoy an *East Anglian Holiday*, tour *The Heart Of England*, head *North To Wales*, relax in the *Lake District*, roam across *Scottish Highlands*, and so on, all easily accessible of course by public transport.

From the technical viewpoint the travelogues were the most difficult films to make because good weather was an essential ingredient. After all who's going to rush to book a ticket for some remote location only seen filmed in wet and dull conditions. The crew experienced long damp days sitting in a shooting brake playing cards during the filming of *The Heart Is Highland* waiting for the rain to stop so the cameras could turn again and show the place at its best.

Not just the regions featured in the travel promo's, but also specific towns and places of interest like churches and country houses. *Glasgow Belongs to Me* (1966) traced the evolution of Glaswegian man from the time the city was a Clydeside hamlet to its twentieth century role as Scotland's industrial heart, with passing reference on the way to some of the City's notable sons, Livingstone, Lister and Watt. Interest in travel could also be generated by looking back at specific historical periods and showing what still remained. This was the theme of *The England Of Elizabeth* (1957), another award-winning production which studied the relics, visible and audible, of Elizabethan England, its castles, houses, churches, jewels, music and plays. Apart from skilful camera work by BTF's own James Ritchie, and an informative script by West Country novelist John Moore, the film had a musical score specially composed by Ralph Vaughan Williams. The unique opportunity for a Vaughan Williams score arose half way through editing. The film had therefore to be given a rough-cut shape to give the composer timings, and the recorded composed score had to be tailored to fit the picture.

Several of the BTC-owned bus companies ran day trips and longer coach tours, and a few films were even made specifically to highlight the joys of touring by coach. *Coaching Holiday* (1958) removed the veil and amusingly revealed how a coach driver cum guide on a tour of England successfully attempted to create a happy atmosphere among a diverse group of holiday-makers cocooned in each others often trying and testy company for a few days.

BTF's best remembered travelogues were almost all made under the aegis of the British Transport Commission. In those days the films didn't always promote one form of transport as distinct from another, so it wasn't up to British Railways, London Transport or any of the other BTC subsidiaries to approach the Unit and commission the work. Post-BTC things were different as travelogues were commissioned, and mostly by British Railways. One of the last made under the old regime was *John Betjeman Goes By Train* (1962), in which the jovial poet travels through Norfolk by rail enjoying the sights of the countryside. This was one of the BTF/BBC collaborations. A Youth Hostel converted from an old barge would doubtlessly rouse the interest of any local TV news programme; BTF made a 25-minute film out of the event. In *Hostellers* made in 1965 we meet two keen exponents who tell how hostels are run, describe the facilities offered, and recall how they became involved in hostelling. Some films were made to promote ferry travel, *Over The Sea And Fast Away* (1973) made the whole process of taking your car across the Channel as easy as falling out of bed. *A City For All Seasons* (1969), a joint venture between BR, LT and the British Tourist Authority, took a look at life in the capital throughout the year, showing there was something on offer whatever the month. Fairly late on in the BTF era *The Stage is Yours* (1979) looked at Britain as though it were a set on a theatrical stage.

As with *Journey Into Spring* many aspects of nature were included in BTF's travelogues. Another award winner was *Between The Tides* (1958), an exploration of the secret coastal world of cliffs and rock pools along the sea shore. The camera stays behind as the sea retreats after high tide and studies the variety of marine life below the cliffs. Shell fish, crabs, starfish, and periwinkles fall prey to the camera lens while going about their furtive business, until the mighty sea returns and conceals it all once more.

By 1967 BTF had amassed an impressive array of over a hundred awards for its documentaries. Some films had won two or more, *Between The Tides* notched up fifteen, including First Prizes at Venice, Bologna and Cork in 1958. It had also won Best Film award in the Sea and Marine category at the 1960 Monaco Festival, and that year it was nominated for the most coveted prize of all, an Oscar, just as *Journey Into Spring* had been in 1958. It didn't win, but the nomination was honour enough. Seven years later the honour came.

Accolades amid the customary glitter at the Oscars ceremony in 1967 went predominantly to Britain's film industry. *A Man For All Seasons* won the award for Best Film, its star Paul Schofield was voted Best Actor, and Elizabeth Taylor was crowned Best Actress for her part in *Who's Afraid Of Virginia Woolf?*. The BBC won the award for Best Documentary for its controversial offering *The War Game*. Cameraman Paddy Carey had double reason to celebrate after the Hollywood extravaganza. Not only had he filmed part of *A Man For All Seasons*, but he had also filmed and co-directed, with John Taylor, the production which won an Oscar for Best Live Action Subject, British Transport Films' entry, *Wild Wings*.

As with *Journey Into Spring* and *Between The Tides*, the stars of *Wild Wings* had no egos to inflate further by the honour of winning such a prestigious award. They were birds; Chinese Mandarin, African Pygmy Goose and the like, all inhabitants of the Wildfowl Trust sanctuary at Slimbridge in Gloucestershire. In the film the naturalist Peter Scott, founder of the Sanctuary, described the work of the Trust in protecting the lives of some of the rare and endangered feathered species. He had also assisted greatly with editing the film. It's odd that BTF's highest award was won by a film without a direct transport theme, but then that's show business!

To list the composers who contributed musical scores to BTF productions would be like perusing the programme of an international music festival covering all strains of the art. Music which is evocative without being intrusive is a vital ingredient of any film, and music played a part in many BTF productions, especially those made for cinema showing. The Unit did not possess its own sound department and it was quite a laborious process laying sound effects on film. Far better then to have a decently composed musical score by a competent composer. Muir Matheson, who had a long and distinguished career directing music on many British films was of great assistance in his unofficial role of Musical Director at BTF, suggesting composers, as well as arranging and conducting many of the recording sessions. Other noted musical directors who sometimes assisted in this capacity were Marcus Dods and John Hollingsworth. Many talented composers were given commissions by BTF; Doreen Carwithen (*East Anglian Holiday*), Clifton Parker (*Ocean Terminal* and others), Elisabeth Lutyens (*Heart Of England* and others) rub shoulders on the list with composers of the calibre of Edwin Astley, Edward Williams, Kenneth V. Jones and of course Ralph Vaughan Williams. In BTF's 36 years, forty composers contributed scores culminating in 110 different recording sessions. The specially composed music complemented the library music which naturally came cheaper and was used on many films to good effect. But the faith that Edgar Anstey and his team had in the quality of their product touched all the elements which made it, and the music, specially composed or from library sources, was no exception.

British Transport Films was a natural part of post-war Britain where a nation struggling to rebuild after the turmoil of conflict felt justified in creating conditions where public services, including transport, could be held accountable to their customers for the level and standard of service they provided. In recent years we have seen this ethos broken down in favour of a return to private ownership and competition. Who can say whether the pro-nationalisation fervour which greeted the post-war era, conceiving organisations like the British Transport Commission and thereby British Transport Films, will ever return? What will never be in doubt is BTF's legacy of brilliant short films which in the years and decades ahead will serve to remind this and future generations something of what life was like in mid-Century Britain as day by day the link slips from our grasp.

Facing Page Upper **A tour by Scottish Motor Traction coach was the subject of the film *Scottish Highlands* (1953). In this shot the bus has The Road To The Isles all to itself.**

Facing Page Lower **Near Fort William a train cuts across the view of bracken and Ben Nevis.**

The Atlantic Coast Express leaves Waterloo for *Glorious Devon* in the 1953 filmstrip of that name. The train is being hauled by Southern Railway Merchant Navy class loco 35018 'British India Line'.

British Railways was naturally anxious to promote school party travel. The filmstrip *To Norwich And The Norfolk Broads* (1955) joined a school party from Essex on a day trip by Eastern Region from Shenfield.

The girls have a friendly word with the crew of class B1 locomotive
No.61253 while, naturally, the boys examine the loco.

Back in the fifties London Transport commissioned several filmstrips to publicise its range of Conducted Coach Tours. Will Hyde Park Corner ever look so quiet again on a weekday morning?

A tour to Luton Hoo in an LT Private Hire Coach pauses by the church of St John the Evangelist in Lemsford, Hertfordshire.

Britain's rural bus network, or at least the BTC element, was promoted in the filmstrip *The Country Bus* (1960). Tavistock in Devon was the selected location where much activity surrounds the departure of a Western National ECW bodied Bristol double decker. A Western National Royal Blue coach provides a road link to London.

Facing Page
Abinger Hammer in Surrey.
A local landmark,
the little blacksmith,
hammer striking the bell,
is just visible in the clock
tower on the left.

Dorking.
Public transport, in the
shape of an RF single
decker and a couple of
double-deck RTs, still has
a strong presence in this
picturesque Surrey
town.

Facing Page *Farmer Moving South*. The train is about to leave Stokesley on the way to Hartfield on the coldest day of December 1950. Because of the very cold weather, arrangements had to be made by the Hartfield station staff for local farmers to provide additional transport to move livestock quickly from the station to Perryhill Farm, about a mile to the north.

D200, now preserved in the National Railway Museum at York, heads the Hook Continental at Liverpool Street Station for the start of *Travel Game*, a journey into Europe through the Harwich-Hook connection.

LIST OF PRODUCTIONS

In the following list, the first column gives the Production Number, the second column the year of publication and the third column the title. Production Numbers 555, 612, 696, 786, 985, 1013 were used twice for altered and retitled versions of basically the same film.

1	1950	TRANSPORT
2	1950	BERTH 24
3	1951	WORK IN PROGRESS
4	1951	THIS YEAR LONDON
5	1950	MOVING HOUSE
6	1951	THERE GO THE BOATS*
11	1953	WASH AND BRUSH UP
16	1950	INLAND WATERWAYS*
23	1951	TRACK BUCKLING AND ITS PREVENTION
43	1952	OCEAN TERMINAL
44	1952	TRAIN TIME
46	1952	JOURNEY TO THE SEA
47	1952	HEART IS HIGHLAND
49	1951	OUR CANTEENS†
51	1951	DAY TO DAY TRACK MAINTENANCE – PART 1
51a	1951	DAY TO DAY TRACK MAINTENANCE – PART 2
53	1951	SAFETY ON THE TRACK†
56	1952	FARMER MOVING SOUTH
57	1952	JOURNEY INTO HISTORY
60	1953	THEY HAD AN IDEA
62	1951	HALLADE TRACK RECORDER
63	1951	MECHANICAL RAIL CREEP ADJUSTER
64	1951	CINE GAZETTE No.9 (OPEN HOUSE)†
67	1953	THIS IS YORK
68	1953	PLACE IN THE TEAM
70	1952	CHANNEL ISLANDS
71	1953	SCOTTISH HIGHLANDS
72	1952	AWAY FOR THE DAY
75	1953	POWER SIGNAL LINEMAN†
84	1951	CINE GAZETTE No.10†
85	1954	MECHANICAL POINT OPERATION
86	1954	WAGONS WITH CARE
87	1953	MORE POWER TO YOUR ELBOW
88	1952	GOOD DRIVING
90	1952	DODGING THE COLUMN
96	1955	BRIDGE OF SONG
98	1955	LAKE DISTRICT, THE
99	1954	LONDON'S COUNTRY†
100	1953	WEST COUNTRY JOURNEY
101	1968	RAIL REPORT No.8 (THE NEW TRADITION)
102	1953	CINE GAZETTE No.11 (SCHOOL FOR SERVICE)†
106	1953	MEASURED PACKING
108	1953	CINE GAZETTE No.12 (THE ELEPHANT WILL NEVER FORGET)†
111	1953	RADAR HELPS SHIPPING
116	1957	EVERY VALLEY
118	1954	EAST ANGLIAN HOLIDAY
120	1954	HEART OF ENGLAND
121	1958	UNDER NIGHT STREETS†
122	1957	FOUR BACK ROOMS
123	1955	MECHANICAL SIGNAL OPERATION
123A	1956	LEVEL CROSSING GATES
124	1956	SAFE TRANSIT
125	1954	WHAT'S IN STORE?
126	1956	MECHANISED RENEWAL OF PLAIN LINE
127	1953	CINE GAZETTE No.13 (CHILDREN'S CORONATION)†
129	1953	CANAL LOCKS AND TUNNELS*
135	1953	DOCKERS AT WORK
137	1950	BOAT TO BIRMINGHAM*
139	1954	RIVIERA HOLIDAY‡
140	1954	LAKE AND LEISURE‡
144	1954	ELIZABETHAN EXPRESS
145	1956	LINK SPAN
150	1954	TEAMWORK OFF THE TRACK
153	1955	CINE GAZETTE No.14 (DO YOU REMEMBER?)†
157	1955	DAY OF ONE'S OWN
167	1955	CAPITAL VISIT
168	1957	OVERHAUL†

No production number was allocated to the last five films listed. The MW numbers are Miscellaneous Works numbers. All dates given are of the year of first publication. Shooting may have taken place some years previously.
*Made for British Waterways
†Made for London Transport
‡Made for Thomas Cook
§Made for Thomas Tilling

YOU'VE READ THE BOOK, NOW WATCH THE FILMS

An increasing number of BTF films
are now available on video.

For an up-to-date catalogue,
write to:

F.A.M.E.
18-20 St Dunstan's Road
London SE25 6EU

BTF videos are available in
specialist bookshops and
all good model stores.